HOW TO MAKE MONEY FROM SOCIAL MEDIA

(FACEBOOK, TWITTER, TUMBLR, LINKEDIN, GOOGLE+, YOUTUBE, INSTAGRAM AND PINTEREST)

TABLE OF CONTENTS

1. INTRODUCTION

2. CHAPTER ONE

    How to make money from Facebook

    How to make money from selling fan page

    How to make money from facebook groups

    How to create a facebook offer for your fans

3. CHAPTER TWO

    How to make money from Twitter

4. CHAPTER THREE

    How to make money from Tumblr

5. CHAPTER FOUR

   How to make money from Google+

6. CHAPTER FIVE

   How to make money from Linkedin

7. CHAPTER SIX

   How to make money from Pinterest

8. CHAPTER SEVEN

   How to make money from Instagram

9. CHAPTER EIGHT

   How to make money from Youtube

   How to make money with your website and promote your business, products and adverts.

INTRODUCTION

This is a step by step guide to how to make money online without any investment. These steps are tested and trusted. Just apply these steps to your social media handles and start making money while having fun.

Many people spend time in chatting on facebook, twitting and even watching videos on youtube for the fun of it. Good news, you can make money while doing all these.

However, with these methods that you are going to learn from this ebook, you can make money while doing what you love to do. Let me take you into a journey of auto money making on the internet.

The first step in making money is to have your own product to sell.

Do a feasibility study on the market. Find important information especially from amazon on products to find what people want and build on it.

Reach out to bloggers and people with an audience in the market informing them about the idea, price and a commission .

Create your product. Build it yourself if you can and have the time or hire freelancers to do it for you.

Build the sales page, conversion funnels, landing pages etc.

Involve bloggers and get them to get traffic your way.

ONLINE BUSINESSES YOU CAN DO WITH YOUR WEBSITE/BLOG

1. You can create a search engine .
2. Start a social media and forum.
3. Start video streaming website.
4. Start a job website or job search engine.
5. Start an online store.
6. Create an affiliate shop.
7. Start an entertainment blog.
8. Start an information resource blog.
9. Start a news website.
10. Create a soccer analysis blog.
11. Start a free classified website.
12. Start a directory website.
13. Create a tech blog.
14. Start a music download website.
15. Start a food blog.
16. Start a freelance website.
17. Start an information marketing website.
18. Affiliate marketing
19. Website and domain flipping.
20. Bulk sms website.
21. Web design website.

HOW TO PROMOTE YOUR PRODUCTS, SERVICES, ADVERTS AND POSTS.

After creating any one or more of websites on the topics above, you then create good content with pictures, videos, infographics and affiliate links. On a regular basis showcase and post good content with valuable information to win over visitors, followers or customers.

You can now move over to the next level, promoting your products and services.

1. Paid Media. Many bloggers promote their products and services through paid media e.g google adwords.
2. Advertise on social media platforms. Use facebook boosted posts, sponsored tweets – engagement tweets, website cards and leads campaigns etc.
3. Youtube ads .
4. Use stumbleupon paid discovery. Paid discovery program puts URL into users streams, directing traffic directly to the page you choose.
5. Linkedin sponsored updates. Create a linkedin company page and also use 'direct sponsored content'.
6. Reddit ads. Promote your content on reddit with promoted posts to target any reddit many communities.
7. Advertise your contents with online publishers.

8. Use paid content discovery services like outbrain, taboola and adblade.
9. Use pay-per-click (PPC). PPC services like google adwords, bing ads and yahoo! Advertising.
10. Guest blog. Search for blogs on your niche and gust blog on them
11. Syndicate your blog. Have your posts and content appear on multiple sites.
12. Get curated. Use services that allows you to distribute the works of others e.g scoopit and paper.li.
13. Encourage comments on your blog.
14. Be social. Use social media following.
15. Use SEO to found on the internet by potential customers.
16. Build an email list. Use newsletter, triggered emails autoresponders series and transaction emails.
17. Social media tricks to promote content.
18. Extract highlights contents and include images to increase stopping power.
19. Include call to action in updates.
20. Use twitter cards which attach media to tweets that link to your content.
21. Share and discuss your content on the most active and relevant linkedin groups.

22. Use +(name) tactic on google+ to ensure your posts are seen by influencers.
23. Pin images on pinterest that links to your website content with rich description.
24. Tag your peers on facebook and various networks that uses tagging systems. Use #hashtags to increase discoverability.
25. Set up and maintain both personal and company profiles and pages.
26. Blog tricks. Integrate your blog with a social style comments section such as disqus, livefyre or even facebook comments.
27. Add social sharing buttons the type that remains on screen as the reader scrolls. Use great images that are worthy to share on pinterest or anywhere.
28. Create prepopulated tweets with the 'click to tweet' plugin.
29. Expand your digital boundary.
30. Youtube – Claim youtube channel and publish video, podcasts and webinars.
31. Cross promote content on your website and blog. Include your website URL in the video description.
32. Slideshare – create informative and entertaining slide presentation versions of your content,

33. Cross promote content on your website and blog,
34. Publish PDFs and infographics,
35. Use Adobe Acrobat to embed links
36. Create a great cover where the title is easily read when presented as a thumbnail.
37. Use Scribd. Scribd has evolved into a library of sorts but it is home to millions of e-books. Joining add to your reach.

CHAPTER ONE

HOW TO MAKE MONEY ONLINE FROM FACEBOOK.

Create a facebook account. If you have an account already, no need to create another except you feel like for this purpose.

Get many followers on your facebook account. Make friends with people of your interest. Targetted audience of the same interest of title or topic of discussion.

Create a community page with a catchy title (Earn $200 weekly on facebook)

Register with affiliate programs (Amazon associates, E junkie, CJ.com)

Write an e-book to sell if you don't have any (Publish with createspace and E junkie or Amazon kindle).

Sell fan pages. Signup with www.shopsomething.com, ensure you have 1000 likes minimum, add your fan page and confirm that you are the owner, set a price and start making money.

Make money by adding adverts to your fan page. Register with www.fanshala.com with your facebook account and pick on available ads. You make money when more people visit your fan page.

Sell Posts or fan pages. Register with facebook posts market or facebook fan pages as an author.

Collect emails with mailchimp by offering a free gift. This is important to get real followers.

Post to facebook automatically with ninja blaster, hootsuite, buffer etc.

HOW TO MAKE MONEY FROM FACEBOOK GROUPS

Create a landing page to collect emails on your website or blog.

Make the landing page to redirect to your online store, an ecommerce store or personal bookstore on website.

Create landing pages with WP Profit builder found on wordpress with links of affiliate offers.

Posts to your facebook groups with ninja blaster or hootsuite

Promote products or links always and target specific niche e.g cooking, photography, writing etc.

Find offers to promote on shareasale, e-junkie and commission junction

Link the offer to your sign up form.

You can create another facebook account for this purpose.

HOW TO CREATE A FACEBOOK OFFER FOR YOUR FANS

Go to your fan page admin.

Click on offer/event+ and select offer from the drop down options.

Select online only offer and use your affiliate link and a discount coupon to offer something useful to your fans.

CHAPTER TWO

HOW TO MAKE MONEY ONLINE FROM TWITTER

Create a twitter account if you don't have one.

Register with kwerdo.com to get affiliate links to post on twitter.

Get more followers by following everyone and anyone in the niche you are promoting.

Use sponsoredtweets through ad.ly, magpie, twitpub or twittad.

Use mylikes, ad.ly, revtwt, twittad, paidtweets.

To get followers on twitter type "followback","follow me","follow for follow","F4F".

Follow anyone and everyone who follows the biggest followback networks.

Follow 200 per day without getting into trouble.

Trending: See what is trending and check what's got the most re-tweets and then just copy what they have said on your twitter. Change it into your own words and do it twice a day.

Tags: Tag 2 posts on things people look at. Look at trends and only tag when I'm posting about trending topics.

Create A Good Twitter Profile

Profile, use (Avatar + Bio)

Use logo nerds

Celebrity followers. Get them to follow you by following them.

Chat with someone. Click on discover and chat with someone of your interest.

Go to trending topics and talk to people there.

Get a twitter queue bot.

Rant. Use a vine and some angry caption text.

Create content with pictures, vines and posts.

NOTE: After creating a good twitter account, getting many followers especially the celebrity followers, ensure to put your affiliate links in every of your posts. Posts regularly and watch your earnings grow. Happy twitting!!!

CHAPTER THREE

HOW TO MAKE MONEY FROM TUMBLR

Create a tumblr account with professional touch.

Register with infolinks, chitika, kontera, viglink, ebates, linkshare to get adverts displayed on your tumblr account and blog.

Pay for uploaded files- rapidgator or depositfiles.

Adding URL or link to other files e.g adf.ly, shorte.st, linkshrink.net.

Upload pictures e.g imagetwist, imagecherry

Use tumblrjazz, an automated way to get followers on tumblr

Use Queue+ to load 2000 images. Set to function for 20 days.

Load up blog

Get chrome extension Archive poster

Go to niche tumblr, URL and add "archive"

Then click "select" and select photos

Then click "Post" and "Queue+"

Go back to Queue+ and set a schedule

The posts are set to run.

Get woozone from wordpress.

Create a good hosted website.

To make on tumblr, go to queue+, click on tumblr blog profile and click edit all post

Put the URL to the website in the caption.

NOTE: You make money from tumblr by the adverts placed on your blog through it by chitika, kontera, viglinks etc.

CHAPTER FOUR

HOW TO MAKE MONEY FROM GOOGLE+

Create a google+ account.

Add target subscribers of your niche of interest.

Create a page in google+ profile about tab.

Include affiliate links of your choice.

Run google+ hangouts.

Create a community. Create your page with a name of your product, also add on "About the product" details

Create a cover pic

Sell your product in your google+ community.

Promote books. Your ebooks or of others.

Increase affiliate products especially in every post

Offer services like freelancing, web design, consulting etc.

Create a blog dedicated to google+

NOTE: You make your by the affiliate links you post and services you offer.

CHAPTER FIVE

HOW TO MAKE MONEY FROM LINKEDIN

Create a linkedin group around an interesting and relevant topic

Use email autoresponder to emails for marketing your products and services.

Add your free giveaway to the publication section of your linkedin profile.

Don't add your linkedin contacts to mailing list.

Add your product under the projects section.

Look for people that hires or needs freelance services.

Look and join groups of your interest

Add books and ebooks to publication section of your linkedin profile (include a link to books on amazon or ebooks on your site or amazon kindle).

Join groups relevant to the topic of the book.

Create a video trailer for your book. Add the video to youtube and then add it as a media element in your linked profile's summary section

Share your blog post of the book to linkedin. Use share button on your site.

Use publication section of your linkedin profile to link to your latest affiliate product review posts.

Join "recruiter network groups" in linkedin (search for job)

Use linkedin advertising.

Use shutterstock for free or paid pictures/photo.

Use hootsuite to post regularly.

Join 50 groups by searching for keywords in the groups search function.

CHAPTER SIX

HOW TO MAKE MONEY FROM PINTEREST

Create a pinterest account and boards that attracts an audience of your interest.

Follow your passion, build an audience and sell to them.

Get followers to your boards and create a mailing list.

Choose a company to promote and ask for sponsorship.

Promote affiliate products.

Create contests on pinterest to sell your own products.

Re-pin other's pins to win an audience and make money.

Make money by teaching pinterest strategies to others by creating and selling ebooks of this strategies.

How To Get Followers On Pinterest

Pin everything and anything you are interested in and create numerous boards for your pins.

Start following everyone that you find yourself interested in.

Add your friends.

Add your friends from social networking sites via the find friends option.

Add products within the fashion and beauty categories. these seems to gain followers the best.

Pin the top products, current fashion and all around useful information.

Use shopsense links and pinterest pins of shopsense.

Use pinwoot.

Use pinterest plugin to your blog.

Use payforyouth.com.

Use keep - for influencers only

Use rewardstyle.

Check boards on money making ideas or earn extra money on the site to learn more about money making ideas.

Check how to earn money online boards, webdesign, blogging, logo design etc.

CHAPTER SEVEN

HOW TO MAKE MONEY FROM INSTAGRAM

Create an account

Post regularly

Take good photos

Use relevant hashtags

Use tagforlikes app

Engage with your followers.

INSTAGRAM AFFILIATE MARKETING

Post attractive images highlighting their products and drive sales through your affiliate URL.

Affiliates- sharesale, ebates, stylinity.

Use bitly.com to shorten and customize your affiliate link.

Create sponsored posts.

Use tapinfluence.

Use Ifluenz.

Sell your photos to twenty20 and community foap.

Promote your business, products and services.

Use Repost for instagram.

Use Infographics plus exclusive offers

Sell your instagram account to fameswap and viral accounts.

Connect with companies- quglu, quickshouts, popular pays, takumi app, snapfluence, instabrand.

CHAPTER EIGHT

HOW TO MAKE MONEY FROM YOUTUBE

Create a youtube account.

Know the type of video you want to upload.

Enable monetization and sign up for google adsense.

Become a youtube partner.

Upload content.

Upload regularly.

Tag your videos with keywords that describe the content.

Gain audience by sending videos out to twitter and facebook, share with people , distribute elsewhere on the internet. Let us go over it once again:

Sign up for Google and setup your own channel.

Buy HD camera and microphone or use your phone.

Get your video and edit it then upload on YouTube.

Advertise on Facebook, Twitter, Reddit, and etc. Use SEO for title search.

HOW TO MAKE MONEY WITH YOUR WEBSITE AND PROMOTE YOUR SERVICES, PRODUCTS AND ADVERTS.

1. Create a website/blog
2. Give your website a catchy title and a good design.
3. Post as many content as possible on your website on the niche of the site and ensure to share them on your social media by placing share buttons on your site.
4. Use auto blog widgets to post on site regularly and easily.
5. Find offers to promote e.g shareasale, commission junction etc.
6. Write e-books to promote on your site.
7. Register with google adsense to start making money monthly.
8. Create space for adverts on your site.
9. Use paid media. Facebook, twitter, linkedin advertising, bing ads, google adwords.
10. Advertise on social media. On facebook, facebook boosted posts. On twitter, sponsoredtweets.
11. Websitecards- good for promoting e-books.
12. Leads campaigns.
13. Youtube ads.
14. Stumbleupon paid discovery.
15. Linkedin sponsored updates. Create a linkedin company page and also use 'direct sponsored content'.

16. Reddit ads. Promote your content with promoted posts targeting any reddit many communities.
17. Publish your content with online publishers.
18. Use paid content discovery services e.g outbrain, taboola, adblade.
19. Guest blog. Write on other people's blog to promote your website.
20. Build your email list e.g getresponse, mailchimp.
21. Use images on your site that are clickable.
22. Create populated tweets with the "click to tweet" plugin.
23. Create videos and post on youtube.
24. Use slideshare to promote your posts.
25. Use pdfs and infographics.
26. Post your e-books to scribd.
27. Sell ad space e.g buysellads, advertisespace, maxbounty, neverblue, peerfly.
28. Create an ecommerce store and link all other of your sites to it.
29. Use ecommercefuel, bigcommerce etc
30. Use content lockers.
31. Create a membership site.
32. Use sponsoredreviews. A site where advertisers pay for a product review.
33. Drive traffic to your site. Send free samples to instagram influencers.
34. Reach out to bloggers and press.
35. Get friends and family to share e.g upworthy.
36. Engage on twitter e.g followerwonk.

37. Write a blog post featuring people with audiences and send it to them.
38. Referral links e.g groupon, swagbucks and ebates.
39. Use your social skills to earn extra money on mashable.
40. Start a popular forum website like warrior forum.
41. Grow your site traffic and sell the site on flippa.

BONUS

MAKE MONEY WITH EMAIL MARKETING

- ✓ Collect email addresses with a popup set up.
- ✓ For individual messages, sell sponsorship.
- ✓ Promote affiliate offers.
- ✓ Create a squeeze page and product funnel using leadpages.
- ✓ Create and sell paid course delivered through email.
- ✓ Attach a sales message on the ''thank you'' page for your email signup.
- ✓ Create and sell highly targeted paid newsletter with propriety content.

CREATE YOUR OWN DIGITAL PRODUCT

- ➢ Write e-books.
- ➢ Set up an email training course.
- ➢ Create a video training course.
- ➢ Create a membership site.

- Form graphics or clipart to sell.
- Create an app or software.
- Create and sell your photography on sites likes istockphoto and bigstockphoto.
- Create and sell audio versions of your e-books using services like ACX.
- Create a digital magazine and sell ads.
- Create and sell small printables like planner pages, patterns and stickers.
- Sell your custom artwork through digital download.
- Create and sell workbook of systems and forms of different businesses.

WHERE TO SELL YOUR DIGITAL PRODUCTS.

1. Sell on your website.
2. Sell on etsy.
3. Build your own store using shopify.
4. Use gumroad.
5. Attach paypal buttons to your site.

MONITIZE YOUR PODCAST

1. Promote your own products and services.
2. Sell affiliate products.
3. Sell sponsored spots through podtrack.
4. Charge guests for appearing.
5. Sell sponsor spots on your show yourself.
6. Divide sales generated by guests' appearances through a special link for the show.

7. Create and offer a premium content membership to get behind the scenes interviews.
8. Create and sell an e-book from interviews you have conducted.

SELL E-BOOKS.

Create and sell e-books on your website using gumroad or shopify.

Sell these e-books exclusively with select or through amazon kdp.

Sell internationally through kobo.

Use Apple ibooks.

Use smashwords.

Use an email signup in the front matter of your e-books.

Send comments on kboards and goodreads.

Advertise your e-books on bookbub.

MAKING MONEY WITH AFFILIATE PRODUCTS

Sign up with amazon affiliate program

Use JVZoo

Sign up with clickbank

Register with CJ affiliate

Use shareasale

Create youtube videos and attach an affiliate link.

CONCLUSION

The above step by step guides are to make money available to you if you apply them on your social media handles. Just ensure you have books, ebooks and affiliates links available to post regularly on your social media handles. When your followers clink on your links and makes purchases you earn. When they follow your ebooks and buy them, your earn. This is a win, win strategy. It is up to you.

For more information and ways to make more money, send inquires to godwinstar2004@yahoo.com.

www.ingramcontent.com/pod-product-compliance
Lightning Source LLC
Chambersburg PA
CBHW070427190526
45169CB00003B/1448